STORIES OF THE BIBLE

STORIES OF THE BIBLE
Noah's Ark

Drejervej 15,3 DK-2400 Copenhagen NV, Denmark
Tel.: (+45) 3531 0330 Fax: (+45) 3531 0334
E-mail: info@scanpublishing.dk
Website: www.scanpublishing.dk

Printed in China
Design by Ben Alex
ISBN 87 7247 771 7 (Hard cover)
ISBN 87 7247 767 9 (Soft cover)

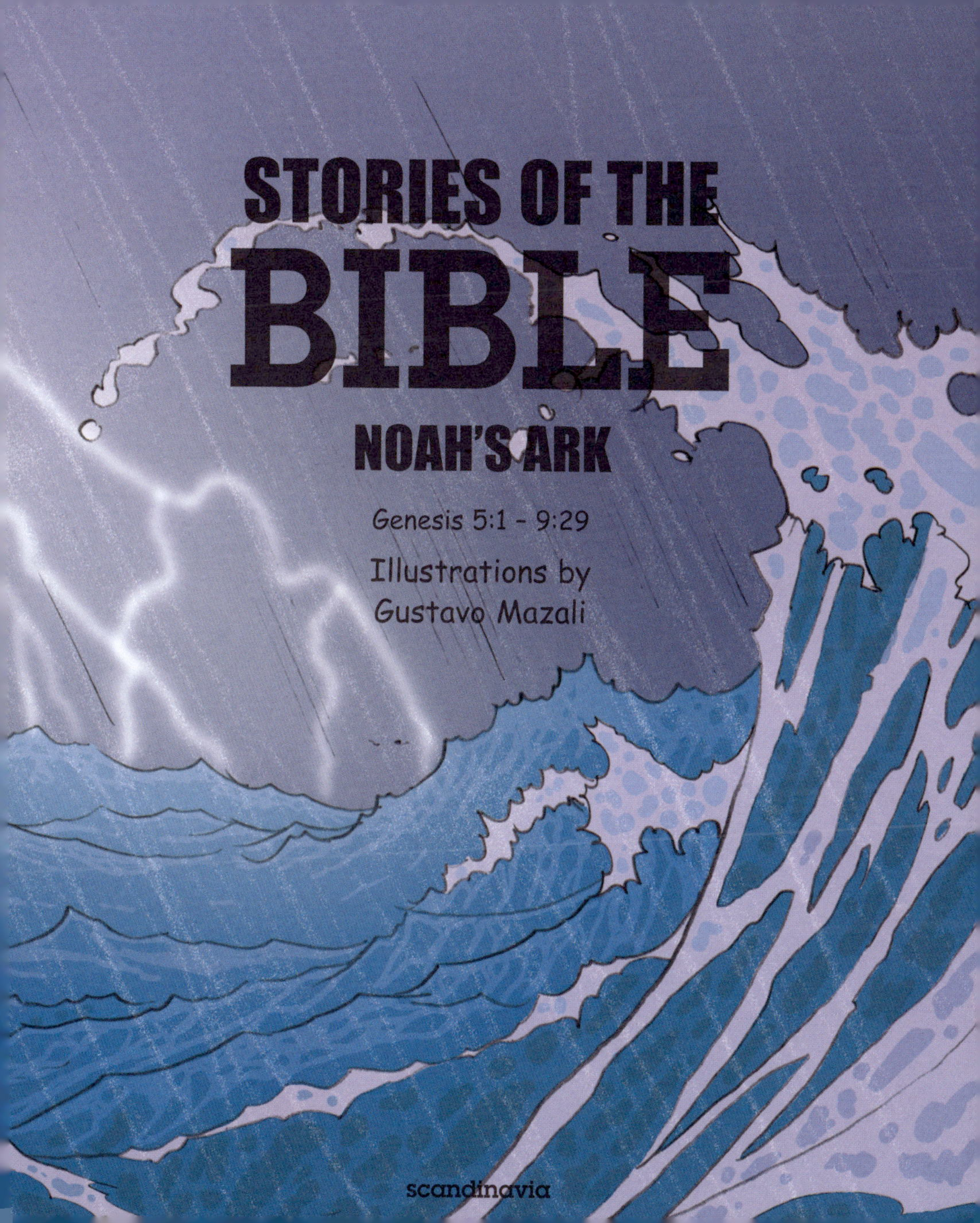

STORIES OF THE BIBLE

NOAH'S ARK

Genesis 5:1 - 9:29

Illustrations by
Gustavo Mazali

scandinavia

Evil people

God looked at the earth and saw how evil people had become. He felt sad because He wanted people to be happy and loving towards each other. So God decided to start all over again—with a man called Noah.

God tells Noah to build a boat

Noah was a good man. He loved God and wanted to do what God told him. Now God told him to build a boat.

"But there's no water around!" said Noah.

"You wait and see," said God. "I have decided to destroy the earth in a heavy rainstorm. You will soon need a boat."

God also told Noah to bring animals into the boat.

"You and your family and all the animals will be safe in the boat," God promised.

The rainstorm

Then it started to rain. Soon the water covered all the houses and high places where people were trying to escape the flood. Only Noah's boat was left.

The rain went on and on until the whole earth was covered with water. But Noah and his family and the animals were safe in the boat.

Inside the boat

It rained for forty days. In the meantime, Noah and his family were busy taking care of the animals.

Then the rain stopped. But Noah stayed on the boat for a long time until he thought the water had finally disappeared.

Noah sends out a dove

Before Noah let out the animals he wanted to be sure it was safe to get off the boat. So he sent out a dove. The dove came back with a green leaf. Now Noah knew there was dry land. It was safe for the animals to get off the boat.

God's rainbow

The animals spread out on the face of the earth, and Noah became the father of many people. God was happy and promised Noah never to destroy the earth again. As a sign of His promise He put a beautiful rainbow in the sky for everyone to see.

The rainbow reminds us that God loves us very much.

Noah's Ark in the Bible

The LORD then said to Noah, "Go into the ark, you and your whole family, because I have found you righteous in this generation. Take with you seven of every kind of clean animal, a male and its mate, and two of every kind of unclean animal, a male and its mate, and also seven of every kind of bird, male and female, to keep their various kinds alive throughout the earth. Seven days from now I will send rain on the earth for forty days and forty nights, and I will wipe from the face of the earth every living creature I have made."